Parrot Fever

Parrot Fever

Joe Rosenblatt

collages by

Michel Christensen

Toronto

Exile Editions

2002

This edition is published by Exile Editions Limited,
20 Dale Avenue, Toronto, Ontario, Canada M4W 1K4

Sales Distribution:
McArthur & Company
c/o Harper Collins
1995 Markham Road
Toronto, ON
M1B 5M8
toll free:
1 800 387 0117
(fax) 1 800 668 5788

Composition & Design by *Michael P. Callaghan*
Typeset at *Moons of Jupiter Inc.*
Joe Rosenblatt Photograph by *John Reeves*
Michel Christensen Photograph by *John Reeves*
Printed and Bound by *Transcontinental Printing*

The Canada Council for the Arts since 1957 | Le Conseil des Arts du Canada depuis 1957

Ontario Arts Council
Conseil des arts de l'Ontario

The publisher wishes to acknowledge
the assistance toward publication of
the Canada Council and the Ontario Arts Council.

ISBN 1-55096-566-2
Printed in Canada

I.M.
Gordon Rosenblatt

FROM PYTHON TO PARROT

With *Parrot Fever* Joe Rosenblatt "regales us with yet another canticle" from dreamland.

The line is borrowed from the second of the XVI sections making up a long poem, each of which is a superb tableau of fantastic images that coalesce, dissolve and re-emerge, shifty as mobile targets in a Luna Park shooting gallery. Those images come mostly from the animal world where the habitat can be either tropical jungle, or small backyard garden. "A miracle of rare device" Coleridge would say of such startling juxtaposition. There we find a wrathful parrot, a snake, felines, birds, frogs — "what more could a dyspeptic (reader) desire in a fantasy?"

As in other poems, animals are often this poet's aliases, metaphorical interpreters of some truth. "What is the truth?"—Nietzsche once asked himself—and his answer was: "a mobile army of metaphors." That's exactly what the poem is.

The leader of such an army is a belligerent grey parrot, later baptized Tuco. The feathered creature, in a way, fathered the poem: the bird was disturbed in his sleep by an unaware Rosenblatt who was passing by the cage on the way to bed holding a glass of precious double malt with reverent care. The bird's ear-piercing protest triggered a reaction that transformed the domestic incident of a spilled drink into a metaphysical experience, and a common specimen of grey West African parrot into the shining messenger of primeval cave dwellers.

Now let me outline a profile of this bizarre creature from the World Below, the Antipodal Land as Huxley used to define the unconscious:

First Name: Tuco
Family Name: Pyttax
Age: astronomic time
Place of Birth: the poet's right frontal lobe
Genealogy: to Darwinians, a descendant of reptiles. To creationists, the emanation of a divine mind, meant to offer men a worthy interlocutor.
Curriculum: none that one knows. If any, it must be ante-litteram, and anti-litteras as well, if I'm allowed the pun. Tuco in fact is no champion of *belles lettres*, judging from the language he speaks. He is a talking animal for sure, but not in Aesop's way. He is neither Aesopic, nor Ethiopic (he comes from West Africa), nor erotic, but simply exotic.
Habits and Manners: most of the times he appears to be an ill-tempered, obstreperous, peevish Pyttax, downright "cattivo," as Italians would say, probably because he's being held in captivity. He is also a radical individualist. Against intruders, he shrieks out his Declaration of Independence in Pyttaceous language. Other times he adopts conciliatory, friendly manners: (*his eyes fix directly at me in sparkling amiability*), or he may even show an ingratiating mood of complicity and ribald camaraderie: (*go pour yourself another healthy drink . . . and pour me a shot in a thimble, but go easy on the ice . . .*) Still other times he plays the capricious child, who demands a bedtime story.

It's hard issuing Tuco an Identity Card, which is much to the satisfaction of the "*ruffled grey parrot craving anonymity.*" Those who would like to know more, may refer to Joe's Id.

As I said, a little domestic incident flung open the doors of inner perception letting in a host of Shadowshapes. They brought voices from the Cave Below, and how, since then, the language resonates! Once, in an interview, Barry Callaghan declared that the one thing that interested him in language was resonance. In this respect, *Parrot Fever* is really a huge audi-torium, full of chants, appalling cries, ululations, howling winds, rhapsodic rhythms, hellish squalls, shrieks, growls, hisses, buzzes, whistles, warbles, whispers . . . octave after octave of preternatural sounds. Resonance, obviously, mustn't be intended simply in a literal way, associated only with the acoustic sense of words, but with the vast evocative aura they create. Conductor Rosenblatt is no novice at audiovisionary experiences, and knows the right procedure: a ceremony in the first place, and attendant rituals complete with ceremonial bowl and sacred dance around a fire.

The ritual is meant "*to free the primal savage / struggling beneath the plaster of his painted psyche.*" A wise thing to do is to exorcise the Ur-Beast and its fellow inmates. Once free to wander at will in their territory, they are now cornered, chained, silenced and have turned into illnesses. Jung was the first to use this definition to indicate repressed unconscious forces, and we may wonder if Rosenblatt was aware of it when he used the term "Fever" in the title, and if he knew that his desire "*to free my oppressor, fling open his little prison door*" was a therapeutic act. This reminds me of a poem by R. Graves, "Outlaws," where tribute is paid to the Old Gods held in chains, "*tamed to silence, shrunk to mere bogey things / who spoke with thunder once at noon / to prostrate kings…*" They are greedy creatures, "*starving for unpaid dues.*" As long as they are denied their due, they'll always be our secret illnesses and nightmares. In dreams or sudden apparitions they come for the ransom, stirring wonder and fear: "*Have we met before in another life? / I cry out in my undulating sleep / while their happy faces reappear / to devour a delicious dream.*" Each visiting shadow clings to life, almost vampire-like: "*I believe he craved my sap for some refreshment.*"

As the reader wanders in the host country of ghosts, he may wonder what it feels like to plunge all of a sudden into the realm of Absolute Beginnings, the Urgrund, as Mircea Eliade called the sphere of the unconscious. Only the saint, the dreamer, the lunatic and the poet may visit the Cradle of the Invisibles, but only poets have the gift of recreating the vision for us to share, so we must be grateful and thank Rosenblatt for inviting us to his mytholyrical banquet. Having thus fulfilled our obligation as polite readers, we must return to the exotic bird.

Now we are in for a real spin when we realize that Tuco, the product of vision, is himself a visionary! We realize he's gifted with second sight when, running into a snake, the parrot thinks he sees in the reptile *"his father's noble mien,"* and *"his mother's smile, supplanted on a serpent's restive lips..."*

Intrigued and enraged, Tuco exclaims: *"No more genetic engineering, no more grand experiments . . . Damn your genome!"* He was wrong. He should have blamed collective memory instead, Psychic Pangea, where everything mixes, merges, interchanges.

What a story, this Python-Parrot confrontation is in section X: it's a climax and turning point that introduces in section XI another story, a real narrative this time. The narrative is a fable, and if we are expected to believe V. Propp, "The next step after the myth is the fable, or folk tale, or legend."

In *Parrot Fever* we recognize the pattern of transformation and the story of the valiant prince, or a handsome youth who, trapped inside an ugly animal, is bound, in the end, to recover his former self through an act of love, usually the kiss of La Belle. *"Set me free, cries a voice trapped inside that* [the frog's] *prideful chest."* Thus far the tale follows the classical tradition, but soon after the pathway diverges leading us into a more or less "tachiste," typically Rosenblattian panorama. The main elements of the fable remain but the story disappears, like the Cheshire cat in *Alice in Wonderland* that vanishes leaving its smile hanging on air. We start being aware of the difference through an important verbal clue, the qualifier "prideful." Incidentally, we remember a similar use in another poem, "The Drowning," where a frog is similarly defined as "a lump of pride". The proud Batrachian, conscious of the spell, shuns the princess' seductions, her gilded stately bed and refuses "*to find employment as a toy.*" Despite some obvious hesitations, the frog gives us a lesson in Stoicism. He will keep to himself, independent and regally aloof , satisfied with his froggy Self and with his role of green baritone, by which he secures the rain and the fertile, *sacred mud.*

To be aware of the spell means, by extension, not to be fooled by life's seductions and snares, by appearances and false pleasures. What more could a dyspeptic (moralist) wish in a fantasy?

Proud, solitary Rosenblatt didn't go the way-of-all-flesh. I'd say he preferred to go the way-of-all-fish.

— Ada Donati

Parrot Fever

I

There was a storm inside my head.
The wind was howling in the night.
A crazy parrot was shining in my mind.

Fluttering brightly in his silver cage
an undraped demon pumped his wings
in sync to a dance on a swinging trapeze.

His talons flashed like tiny crescent daggers
while a distant cry mocked my racing heart
and pursued those heartbeats for a meal.

I saw the timorous snail of a cryptic tongue
flicker from his lethal beak; swaying in a trance,
Bedlam's bird stomped his profane feet

to the untamed beat of a carnivore's chant
exalting torn flesh and shattered bone
scattered beneath a hemorrhaging sunset.

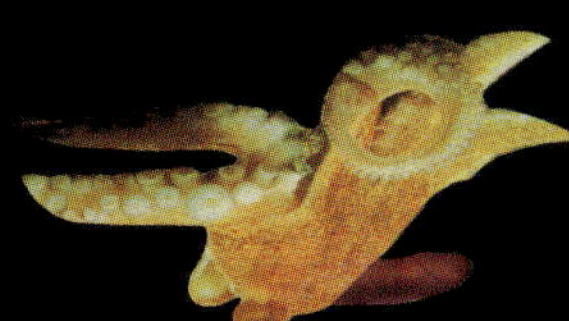

II

Before me I beheld a disquieting tropical oddity
in exile from some haven for the criminally alien
for each icy eyeball betrayed a tormented comedian.

Having blighted his window by my sinful visit
this crooner with a corkscrew for a voice, Tuco
regaled me with yet another canticle from hell.

His primal jungle ululation, a seismic weapon
jarred my hand splattering my precious liquor
which slowly trickled across the weeping table.

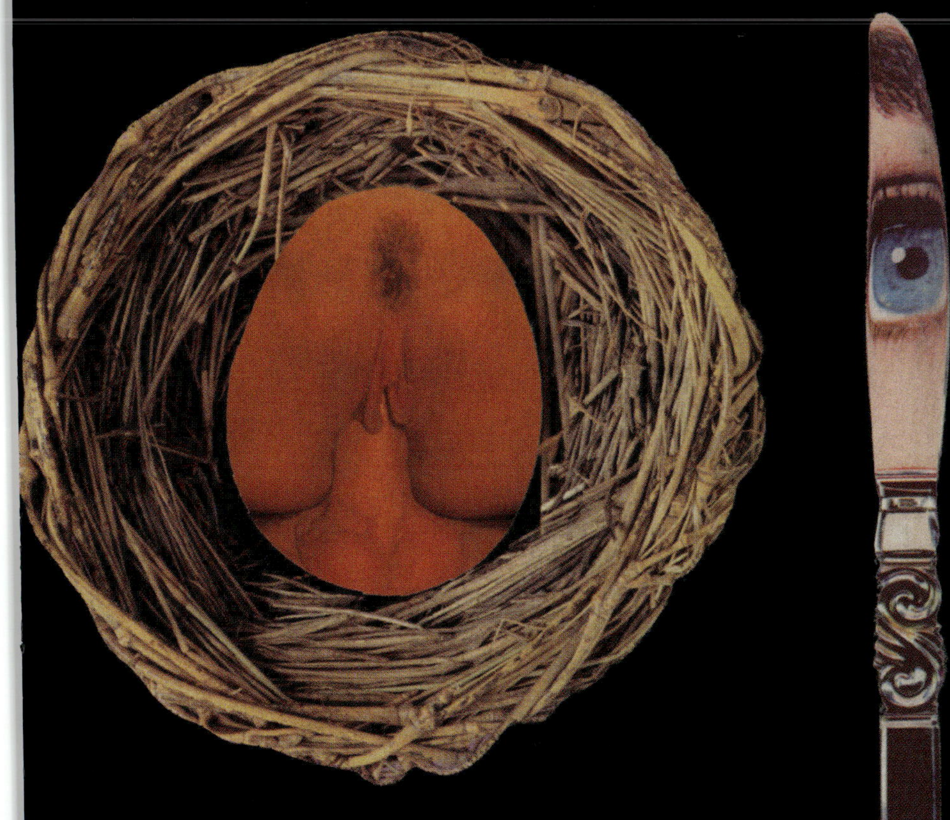

Enraged, I turned to curse my twisted oppressor
just as this tsunami of a whistle swept into my bones
to lewdly freeze and chill that sunny fabric

forming the hairpiece of my afflicted soul
turning the iridescence in those damaged ringlets
titanium white, before fading to a sickly alabaster.

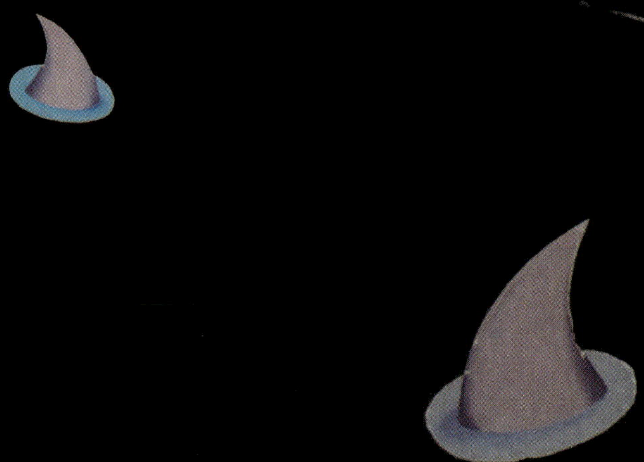

Tuco puffed out his chest in a magisterial huff
which ruffled the calm of his slate-grey feathers;
enhanced by dementia, how that plumage shone!

III

A vengeful tippler's hour finally arrives
when a mythic egg is gleefully cracked open . . .
its captive yolk swept into a ceremonial bowl

and vigorously aerated for a royal omelette.
Giddy, the souse inspired by a whirlpool, in miniature,
as glorious retribution for a precious drink, violated!

An exotic egg, desecrated, and my heart soaring
for by this ritual, I yearn to free the primal savage
struggling beneath the plaster of his painted psyche:

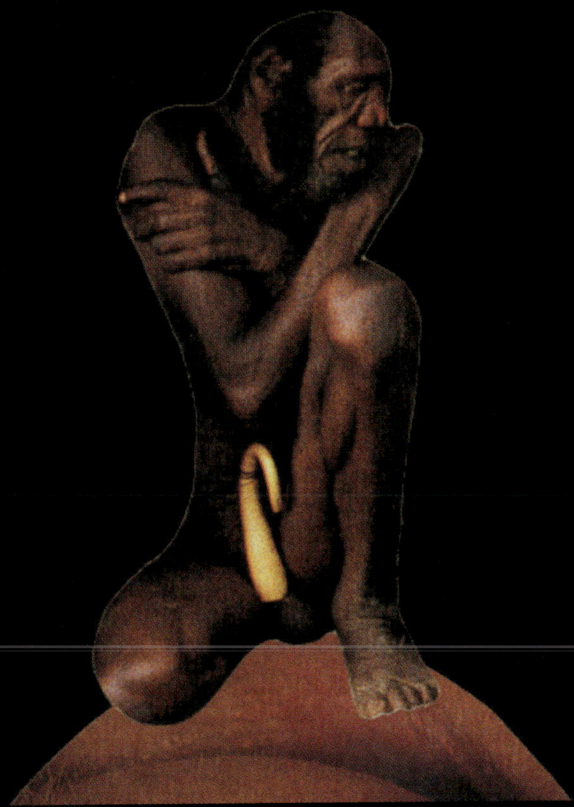

to liberate this beast longing to join a forgotten tribe
encircling the flames leaping deep inside a cave
spiralling, wild in ochre, black, blue, and red

moving as in a trance under stalactite and hanging bats.
Oh, this is not some pretty waltz, but a sacred dance
since everything that feeds, must first feed upon itself.

Indulging a famished dialectic in the viscera of history
Tuco meditates on the speculative taste of an aged bard
and suddenly a dismissive glow issues from his beak.

Driven by the rhapsodic rhythm of his claws
he reacts like any bored sanguinary emperor
dismembering a hedonistic guest at a banquet

although Tuco wouldn't need a lethal beak or claw
to cut through any bone, you see he has a song
whose pitch would pierce a zombie's *medulla oblongata*.

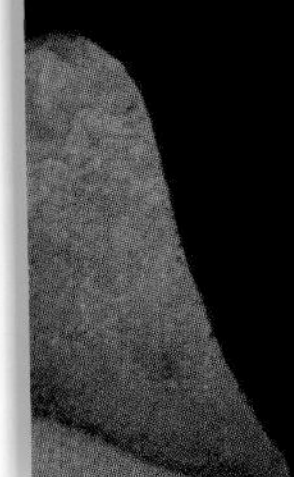

IV

At some mothy hour on a drowsy farm
a russet-coloured cat asleep by the stove
suddenly stirs, and springs out of a nightmare

his languid brain fried by a sudden squall . . .
spooked, a once-spirited pet, now a damaged animal
stares at the sky, entranced by those twinkling mice.

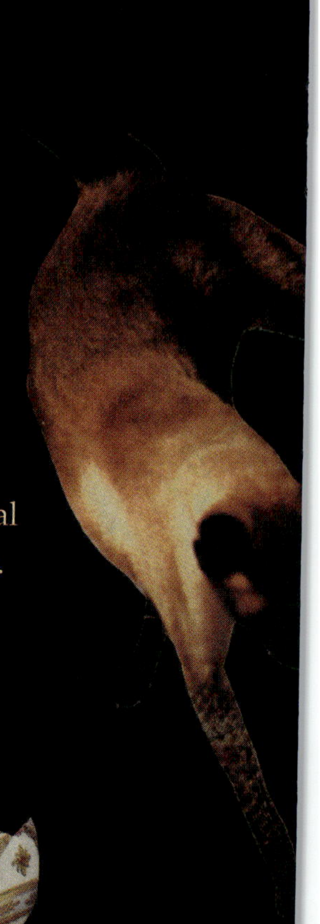

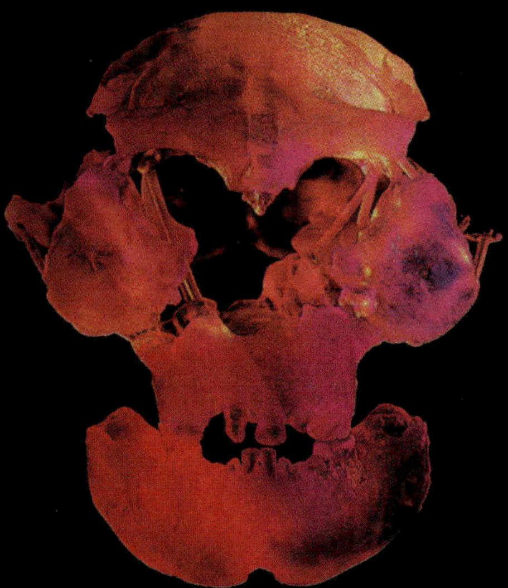

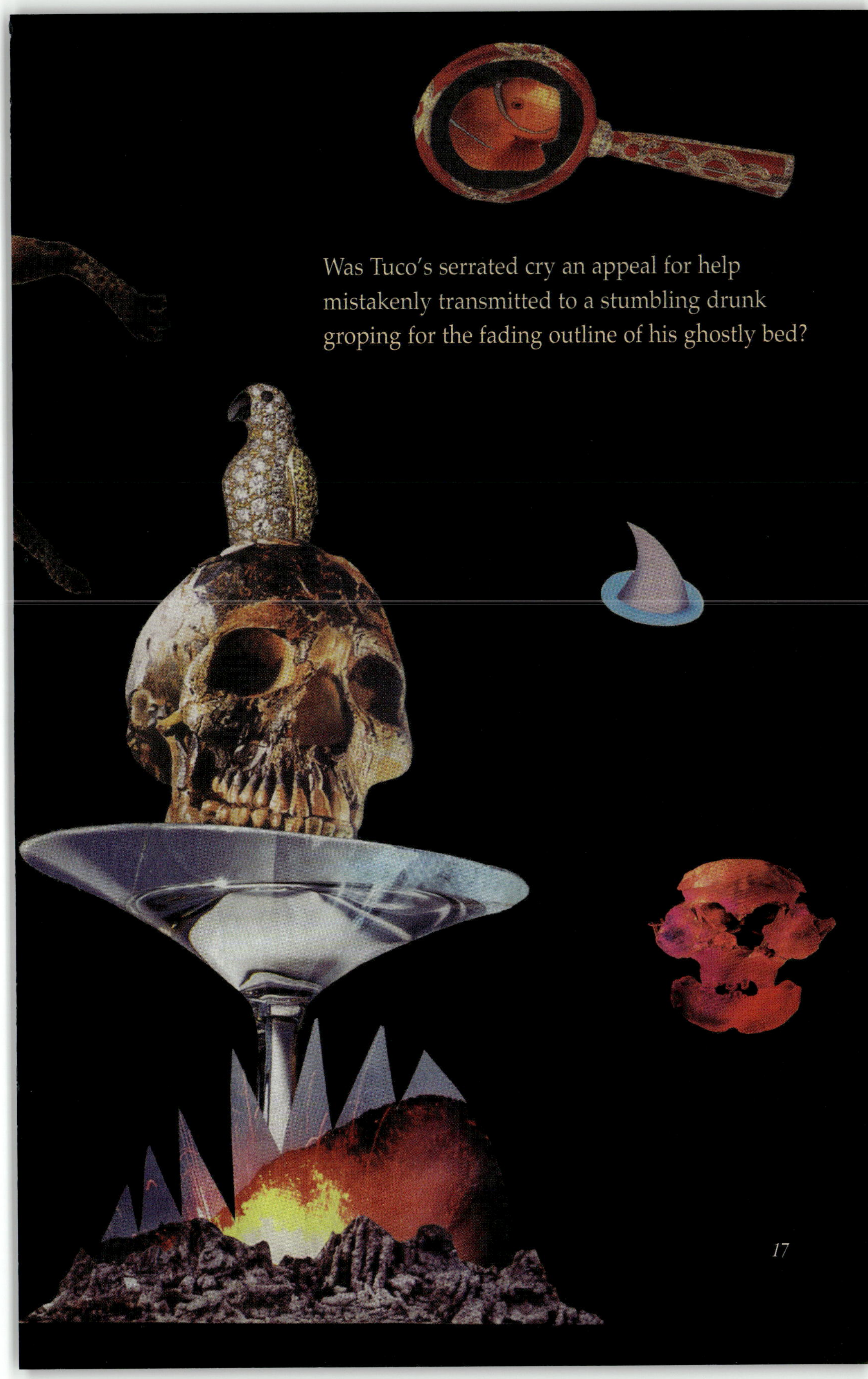

Was Tuco's serrated cry an appeal for help mistakenly transmitted to a stumbling drunk groping for the fading outline of his ghostly bed?

Laved in a delicious luminosity, full and bright,
I seemed to levitate in that room, and giddy
in the toxic light, I desired to free my oppressor

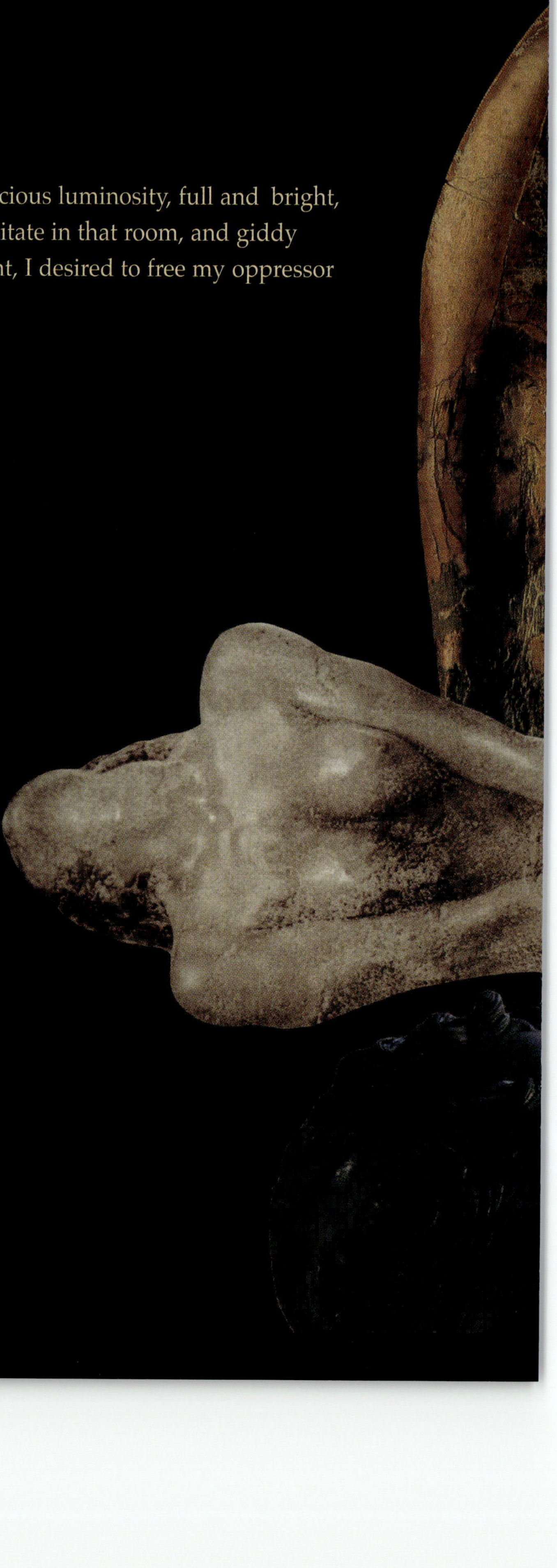

fling open his little prison door, and direct him
to an open window to find his camaraderie of lunacy
and other unhinged associates who'd molest

a summer's evening . . . attacking a vole or a guest
drinking his blood for a nightcap, or for a thrill
scrunch on a femur, straight through to the marrow.

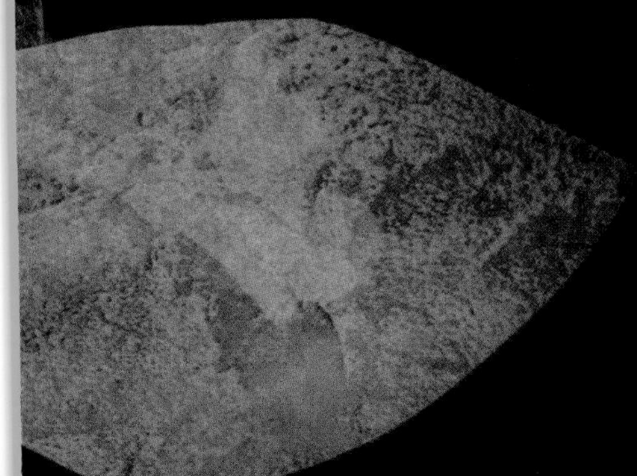

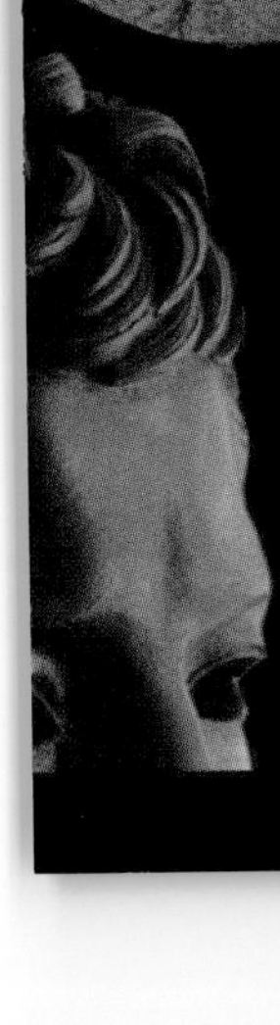

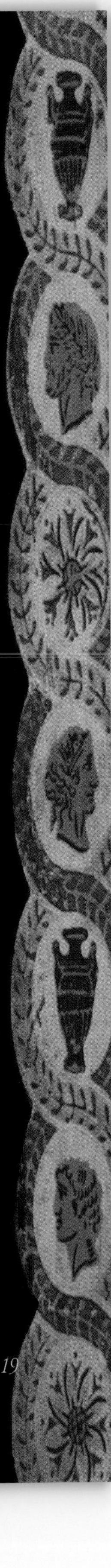

His sagacious eyes belied dark inkwells of loathing
for I believe he craved my sap for some refreshment.
Ah, but it seemed so sensible to convey one's libation

to an awaiting pallet, and there by bibulous degrees
fortify his soul, and secure intact, his precious slumber
by offering his pickled brain as a pillow to Morpheus.

I was in need of a soothing heavenly potation
although in desperation I'd have turned to wormwood;
instead, I carried my evening drink carefully, slowly

mindful that each drop was a jewel shining in the dark.
My one desire, to close the hatch of my submersible
and sink like some crustacean into a sediment of sleep.

V

I knew a man who trained a crow
to make those sounds that parrots make
when they fixate on a cat's meow

or hear the distant timbre of an infant's cry.
Spectres fleeing into a wintry sky,
shapes I desire yet cannot touch

fly through the gloomy ether of my mind
their dark wings flutter and glide across
the horizon high above a brooding sea.

Prancing hypnotically in his cage
splenetic Tuco shrieks out a family secret
embellishing his revelation with a curse

while in the garden conversant ravens
chase away a few intrepid sparrows
to pounce upon some discarded cat food.

VI

Glaring at me as through a shroud
each apparition slowly filters through
for an entertaining visitation.

"Have we met before in another life?"
I cry out in my undulating sleep
while their happy faces reappear

to devour a delicious dream.
Mouths growling at the moon
combust into a final song.

My geriatric cats are always famished
since they keep forgetting they've just eaten.
Their souls are always on the prowl.

I see them steal across the lawn.
Yet I won't indulge my playful friends
who sleep by day and hunt by night.

There is a reptilian charm
to some predator in tiny slippers.
In him I sense the optic heat

of a panther in miniature:
a tabby living on the wild side
ogling his dreamy quarry . . . a robin!

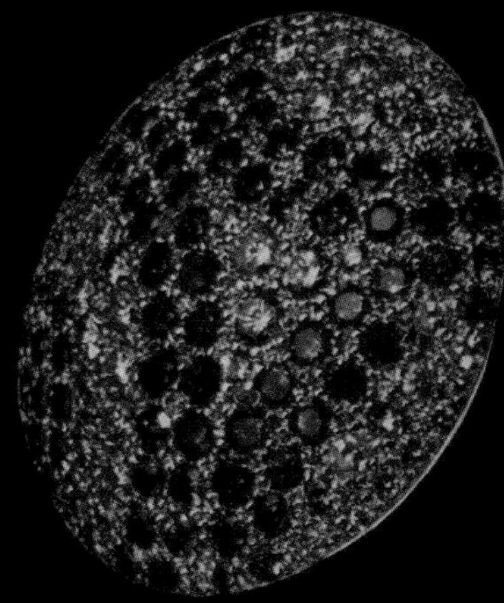

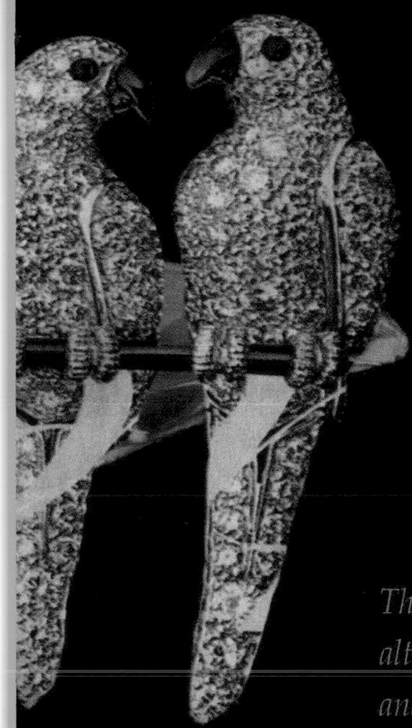

VII

The rain makes Rossella sad
although it makes the fishes happy
and when those revellers are contented

to perform a minuscule iridescent dance
those pulsing teardrops entice a solitary heron
to kiss the surface of the pond, in veneration.

In the evening I watch my cats disappear
dragging their shrilly toys into the darkness
and when the passing heat of fireflies inspires

the stealthy pride by way of a phosphorescent muse
they'll bring some trophy home for me to view:
their eyes invite me to join them in a nocturnal feast.

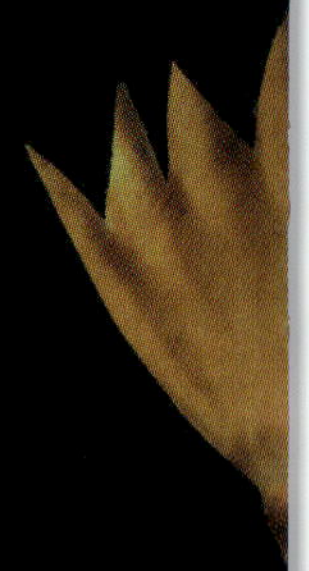

VIII

The rain makes Rossella sad
but it makes the cats so glad
for in singing for their supper

they expect the rain again to bring
a fishy banquet from their Host.
I cannot stop the rain, Rossella

but welcome to this crowded garden
where famished cats, dark and sinister
crouch upon a crooked fence.

The rain is pleased, yet you are sad, Rossella,
although not as gloomy as sepulchral Tuco
incarcerated inside his whistling cathedral.

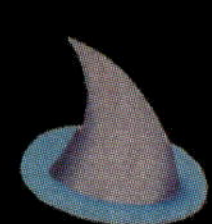

IX

In a wash of indigo,
me and my dying cat escape
into this floating dream

where stellar felines blossom
like petals in a sunny garden
to shine upon an expiring mouser.

In offering these fragile words
I elevate this loyal friend
above the human crowd.

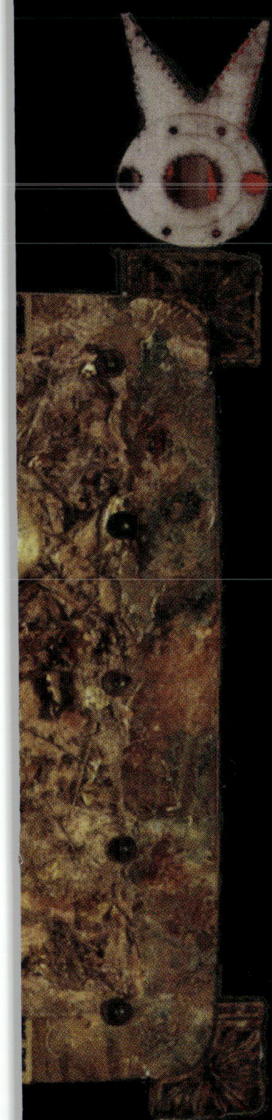

X

Crunching a chicken bone of abstraction
Tuco cackles for his bedtime story
or he yodels to know what lies beneath

the phantasm of all fleecy existence
as concealed within the fluff of a plumy virgin;
he warbles sweetly as though all is forgiven.

His eyes fix directly at me in a sparkling amiability
"Go pour yourself another healthy drink," he cries
"and pour me a shot—in a thimble, but go easy on the ice."

A ruffled parrot craving anonymity
blinks at an expanding serpent inhaling gold:
Tuco sees the traveller slither on the ground

and lengthen out into a tapestry of venom.
The spiral's lacquered eyes glimmer in the light;
a cool jade-green fire dances in each shifting eye

yearning for a trophy frozen on a high leafy bough:
Is he a real bird, or just another shimmering apparition
cooking fiercely in the noonday heat on a jungle floor?

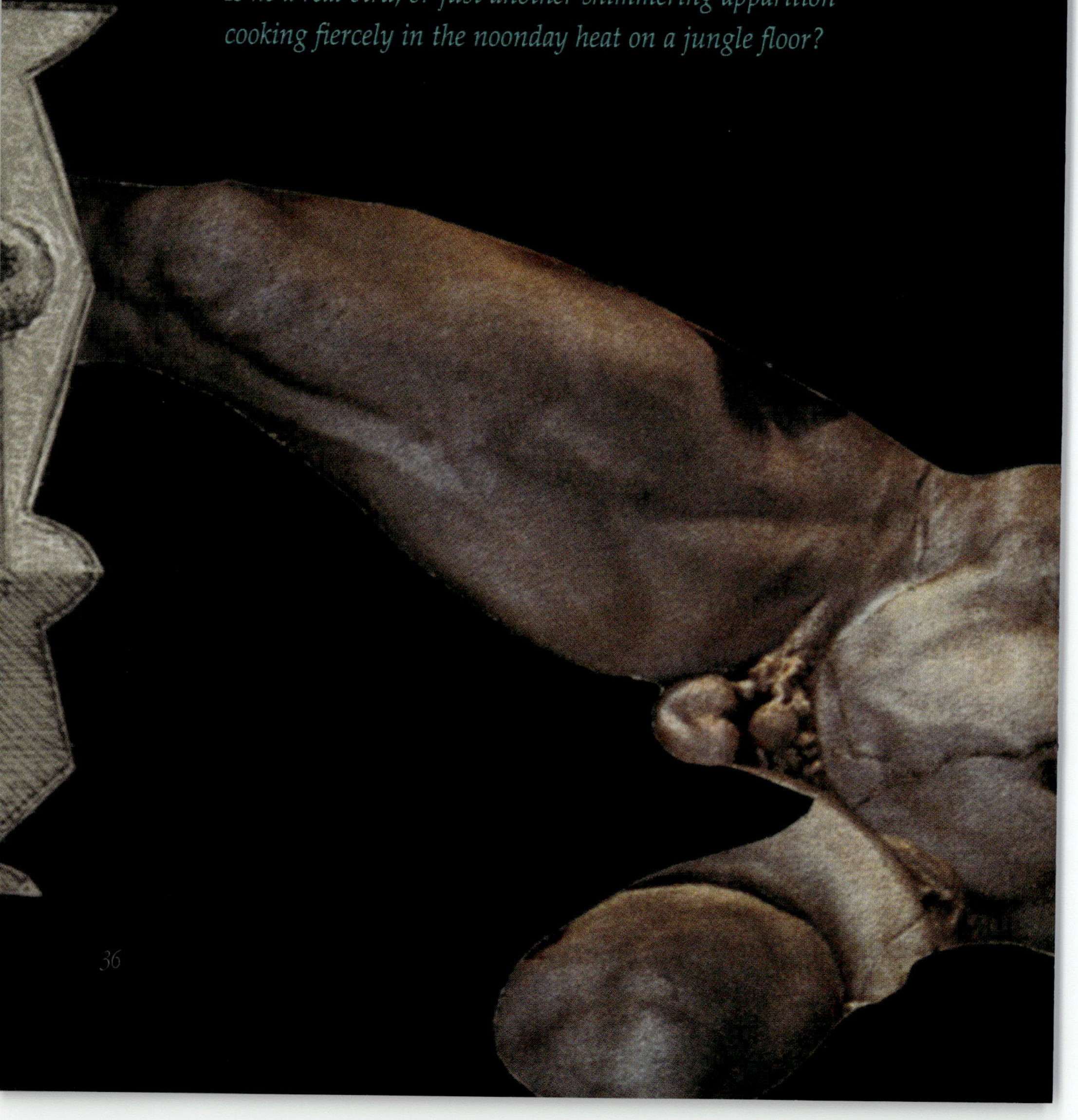

"Have we met before?" trills Tuco, at the palpitating traveller
"I don't believe we've met," declares that sleepy hissing train.
Gliding out of view, a reptile hastens home to a brambly nest

crowded with incubated members of a squiggly shingled race.
Tuco is displeased, for the stranger had his father's noble mien.
Yet worse, he thought he saw his mother's smile supplanted

on a serpent's restive lips . . . fanned by a shameless tongue!
"No more genetic engineering, no more grand experiments"
a beak erupts. "Damn your genome, give me a chicken bone!"

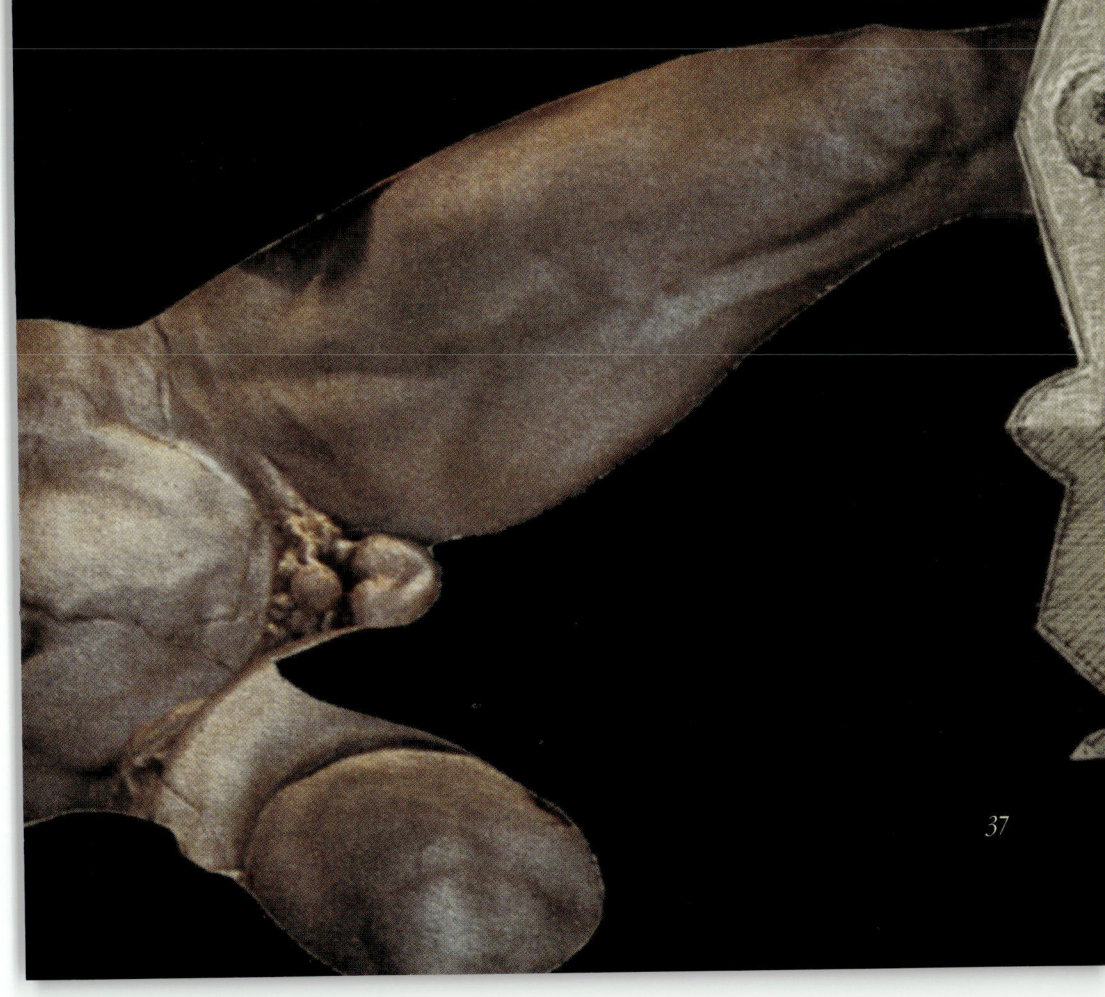

XI

Transformed by a comedienne's wicked spell
into a bubbling verdant baritone, this former prince
emerges blinking from a sunless well.

Compelled to leap at rioting dragonflies at noon
above the brackish water of an ornamental pond
a primo buffo of a frog finds employment as a toy

to gratify the fetishistic urges of a princess;
Love's unwilling prisoner, this tiny naked man,
he can't escape his nightly transport to her pillow

filled with feathers of her father's deranged parrot;
nor can he contain the heat she's ignited in his loins,
or stop the dewdrops flowing from their lustful union.

Yet how to explain his divided self to an addled adolescent
that often he'd prefer the moisture of a bog to her tears
and shun the tantalizing linen on her stately gilded bed?

XII

In a darkened parlour I see an enraptured stranger
reclining on a divan, his webbed fingers reaching
toward a liberating emanation drifting in the room:

embedded on a steely blade, suspended like a poltergeist
a pair of luminescent eyes stare out to transfix a frog;
for what this vixen sees, she'd want in any virile potentate.

In flight, her fingers descend upon his body's green domain.
Aroused, his tensile skin shudders like a tiny throbbing bird . . .
"Set me free," cries a voice trapped inside that prideful chest.

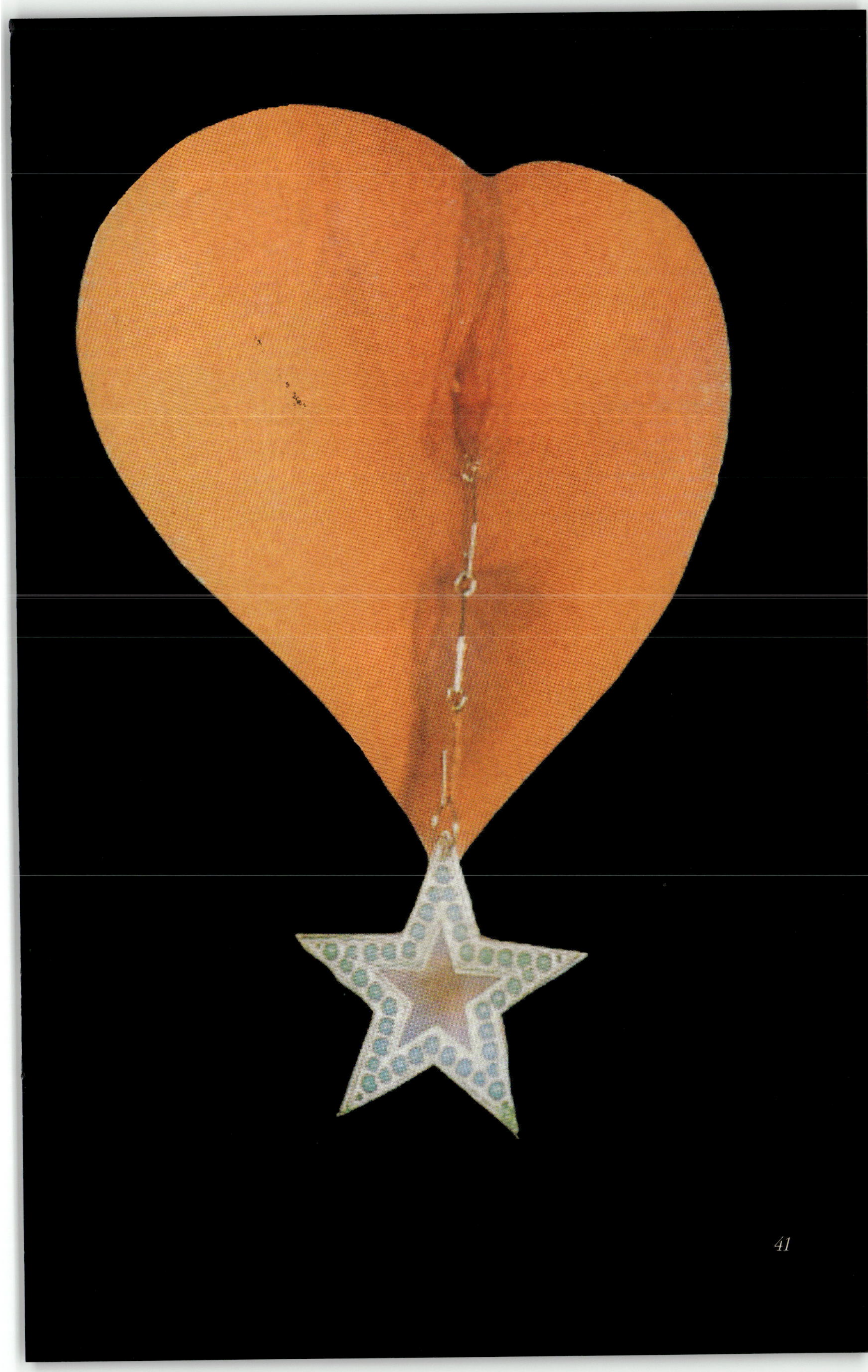

XIII

He sees his deliverance in the opalescence of her eyes
and feels the twists and turns of her desire, to rid him
of his disease, devolve him back to a former prince!

She'll plant a petal of a kiss on his open mouth
but first she'll press him to her swelling breasts
as though he were a flowering orchid, or a child.

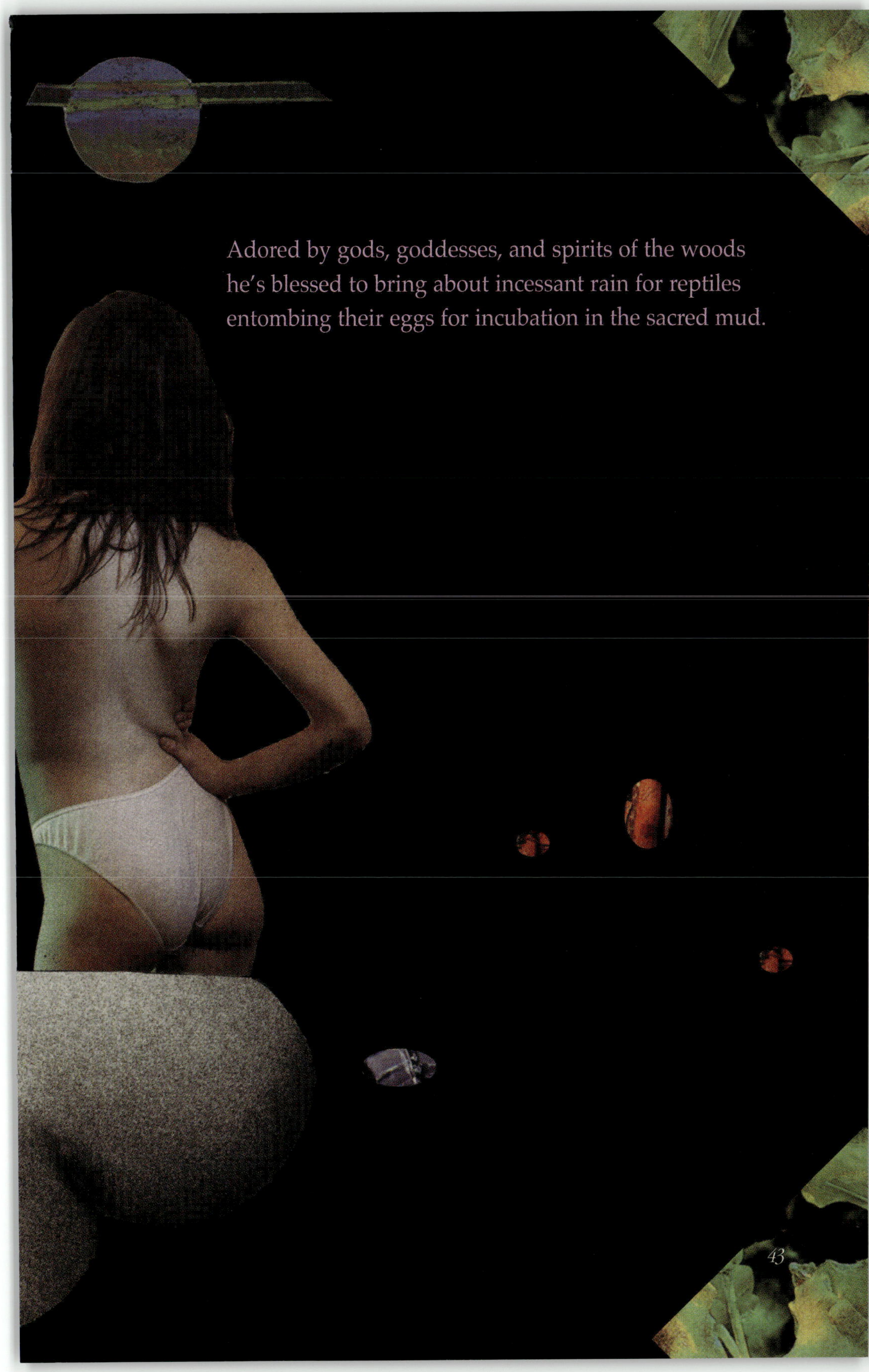

Adored by gods, goddesses, and spirits of the woods
he's blessed to bring about incessant rain for reptiles
entombing their eggs for incubation in the sacred mud.

A warped romance burns like methane flaring in a bog:
an oleaginous lover belches for another recreational kiss
from a princess enjoying her dalliance with an alien.

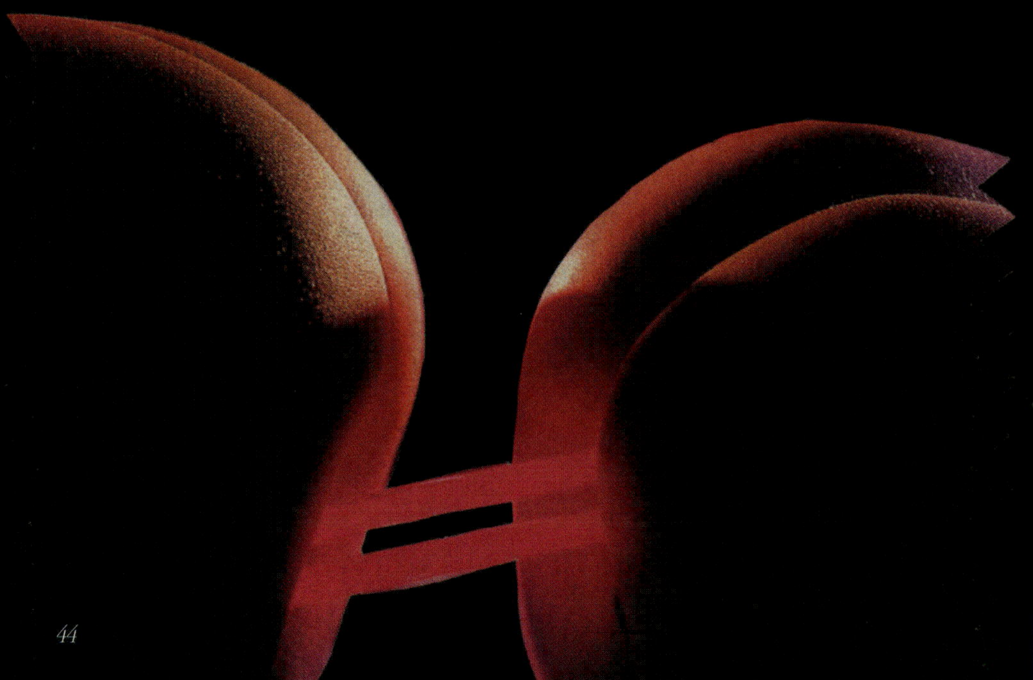

Since batrachians have long preceded clowns and kings
a curse upon the chef who serves this perverted repast:
some *grenouille's* severed leg flavoured in a cognac sauce.

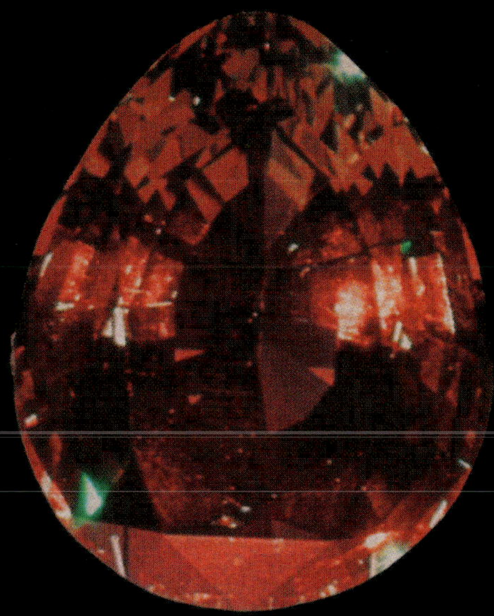

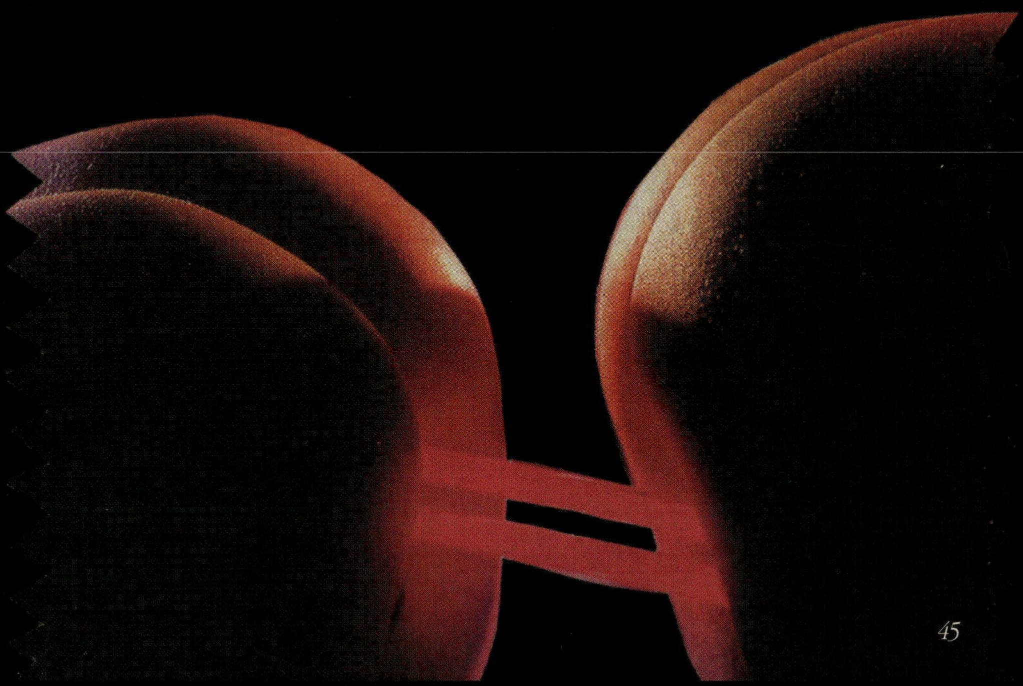

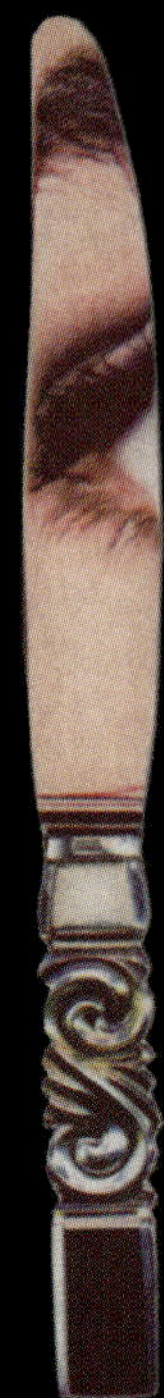

XIV

In the celestial light of a crystal skull, a bedazzled bird
reads my drink of Bombay Gin and ruffles his feathers:
he sees no hope for the bodily resurrection of a parrot!

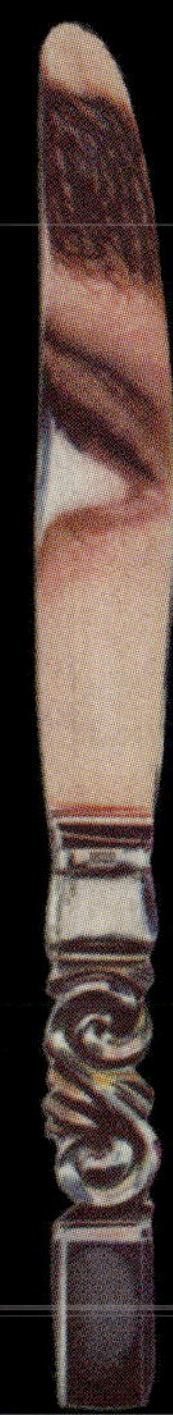

Apostle birds apply their beaks as a collective trowel
to camouflage their nest on a bough of mottled leaves;
so the tropical wren weaves her leafy poem into a nest

honouring the muse of a nearby hive abuzz with wasps
whose devouring songs seep into the mollusc of my brain
troubling my sleep to stir and turn like a snail in its shell.

Redemption, you're that naked lady swinging on a trapeze
though I suspect you were Tuco in a previous incarnation
and now you're his replacement playing in a resplendent cage.

XV

A runaway clock, a fertile fish, a severed egg, and an angel:
What more could a dyspeptic frog desire in a fantasy.
Scantily clad, a cooing princess on an unmade bed invites

a tumescent pet to palpate her firm alabaster thighs
with an amorous tongue swifter than a sunbeam kissing
drunken dragonflies pulsing across a dozy swamp.

He was that little Sunday painter straddling a lily pad
exhausted from making love to some unfinished dream;
—his musky bog, in oil, splashed on a blinding canvas—

Once awakened from a midday nap he saw a shadow
fleeing from a cloud of weeping tadpoles; it was his soul
which sped away from the teardrops of a grieving sky . . .

"I'll catch that dew," he whispered to his tranquil pillow
while he made a plea for the scented lap of his mistress
and as he begged for the soporific rhythm in her hands,

his spirit surged to embrace the expanse of a primeval soup:
attired in purple crocuses, she, a parched mother
awaited the burst of an approaching summer shower.

XVI

In Tuco's piercing eyes I see my mother's scornful gaze:
I believe she was a dusky bird of prey in another life.
I hate that furious god who formed this parrot!

Here's a bird who'd accept a rooster's meatless limb
before he'd taste a debaucher's flesh, sweetly embalmed
in wine, or accented in a fine Dijon honey-mustard sauce.

A fiendish heart lies buried under Tuco's restless bosom
for when again he secures a treasured finger in his beak
my mind freezes as he scrunches an imaginary digit!

Life makes a meal of all of us who move upon the land
or bubble arias in a marsh while we woo some fiery mist
rising like spooks above the night to amuse the living.

Tuco will live a thousand years and go on rattling tipplers
mimicking their curses while they stumble with their drink
into the darkness which he wears for his grim disguise.

REDEMPTION

Joe Rosenblatt

Michel Christensen